MW01616264

Baseball

BALLS & STRIKES

Every Pitch Counts

By Matt Moore

FROM REFEREE AND THE NATIONAL ASSOCIATION OF SPORTS OFFICIALS

BASEBALL BALLS & STRIKES:
EVERY PITCH COUNTS

By Matt Moore, associate editor, *Referee*/NASO
Cover and layout by Rob VanKammen, graphic designer, *Referee*/NASO

Published by *Referee* - Sports Officiating Content
and the National Association of Sports Officials.

Printed in the United States of America.

ISBN-13: 978-1-58208-202-8

TABLE OF CONTENTS

INTRODUCTION

The pitcher winds up and lets go of the ball. The batter doesn't swing. In less than half a second, the ball is in the back of the catcher's mitt. Now all eyes and ears are on the plate umpire.

Ball or strike?

There is no other option. You can't say play on, like a basketball official on a potential block-charge. It's not incidental contact on a possible pass interference in football. There's no advantage rule like in soccer. And there's definitely no "do-over" like in volleyball.

Ball or strike?

There's no boundary line that makes the call clear. You are tasked with determining if a ball, moving at anywhere from 65-95 mph, goes through a three-dimensional space that has no marked borders. Oh yeah, the ball isn't approaching on a straight line, but instead has plenty of spin and break to it.

Ball or strike?

The decision, and the more than 100 exactly like it that occur in every game at every level, is what makes baseball the toughest sport to officiate consistently.

Ball or strike?

Pitchers don't "hit their spot." Batters swing and miss. Catchers receive the ball poorly. All of those mistakes are A-OK. Umpires missing a pitch? It can be the beginning of World War III!

Ball or strike?

You have to make the call. And the way to make the call correctly most of the time is to follow the fundamentals of umpiring — having a proper stance, tracking the ball, having good timing and understanding the actual strike zone. That's what this book will cover, in detail.

In more ways than one, there's never been another book like it. First, no one book covers the art and science of calling balls and strikes. Second, it's the first baseball book published by *Referee* that includes a DVD with video clips that provide enhanced content that supports the written word and graphics.

Ball or strike?

You make the call!

Matt Moore
Associate editor
Referee / NASO

WHAT TO WATCH

Throughout the book, you will see this box. That refers you to the DVD that came with the book. The DVD has material on 17 different topics that are covered in the book. The DVD is intended to be a complement to the book in that using the two together will enhance your understanding of the topic being addressed.

OUR EXPERTS

MIKE DROLL — NCAA umpire for Big Ten, Big 12 and Missouri Valley conferences. Has worked college baseball for more than 30 years, working 11 NCAA Regionals and numerous conference tournaments.

TOM HILER — Has been the Director of Umpire Training for the NCAA since 2008. He is the umpire coordinator for many conferences, including the West Coast Conference (Division I) and California Collegiate Athletic Association and Great Northwest Athletic Conference (Division II). He spent six seasons as a minor league umpire, reaching the Double-A level and umpired college baseball for nearly 20 years. He retired from the field in 2008.

JUSTIN KLEMM — Executive Director, Professional Baseball Umpire Corporation, which oversees umpiring for Minor League Baseball, since 2008. Prior to that, he was a field evaluator and instructor for PBUC for four years. He spent nine seasons as a minor league umpire, and worked 186 MLB games as a vacation/injury fill-in.

DAVID RILEY — A minor league umpire for nine seasons, reaching the Triple-A level for three seasons. Worked three seasons of college baseball, advancing to one NCAA regional before retiring due to job issues. Currently the chief instructor for the Mike Walsh Memorial Umpire Clinic in Indianapolis.

MARK UYL — An NCAA umpire in the Big Ten, Big East and Mid-American conferences. Worked NCAA Regionals for five seasons and also worked two Super Regionals. He serves as the Assistant Director in charge of baseball for the Michigan High School Athletic Association and is a former member of the NFHS Baseball Rules Committee.

ACKNOWLEDGMENTS

I can't thank Mike Droll, Tom Hiler, Justin Klemm, David Riley and Mark Uyl enough for their time and their willingness to share their knowledge about umpiring.

Several people worked on the video that is included with this book. Behind the scenes, there was Mike Dougherty, the multimedia manager for *Referee* and Jeff Stern, the senior editor for *Referee*, who also served as a photographer. The umpires who gave of their time to participate in the video demonstrations were Todd Korth, an associate editor for *Referee*, and Chris Viverito from Villa Park, Ill. Todd, Jeff and Chris are all active umpires. The coaching staff from the University of Wisconsin-Whitewater — head coach John Vodenlich and assistants Justin Bach, Justin Stewart and Shaun Wegner — provided a location and acted as the pitcher, catcher and hitter in the demonstrations.

And last, a thanks to the Michigan High School Athletic Association and Iowa High School Athletic Association for providing video from championship games to add real plays to the demonstrations.

This book is truly a work of many people and it wouldn't have been nearly the product it is without their advice and assistance.

Chapter 1
STRIKE ZONE

T o begin to understand what constitutes a strike, it is necessary to have complete understanding of the strike zone and what constitutes a strike. Take away swinging strikes and foul balls. For now, just focus on the pitches that must be called balls or strikes. An average nine-inning game at the MLB level features around 300 pitches. Of those, around half require a decision by the umpire.

The Definitions

Being one of the most basic parts of a game, it would be logical to think that the definition of what constitutes a strike would be the same among the three major rules codes — NFHS (high school), NCAA (college) and Official Baseball Rules (pro).

Unfortunately, they are not the same, and while the differences may be slight, that can only add to the confusion that is created.

Here are the definitions out of each rulebook:

NFHS: The strike zone is that space over home plate, the top of which is halfway between the batter's shoulders and the waistline, and the bottom being the knees, when he assumes his natural batting stance. The height of the strike zone is determined by the batter's normal batting stance. If he crouches or leans over to make the shoulder line lower, the umpire determines height by what would be the batter's normal stance.

NCAA: The area over home plate from the bottom of the kneecaps to the midpoint between the top of the shoulders and the top of the uniform pants. The strike zone shall be determined from the batter's stance as the batter is prepared to swing at a pitched ball.

PRO: The strike zone is that area over home plate the upper limit of which is a horizontal line at the midpoint between the top of the shoulders and the top of the uniform pants, and the lower level is a line at the hollow beneath the kneecap. The Strike Zone shall be determined from the batter's stance as the batter is prepared to swing at a pitched ball.

Width of the Zone

The first step of determining the zone is figuring out the width of the zone. Regardless if the batter is 6-foot-6 or 4-foot-1, the width of the zone doesn't change. But how wide is the strike zone? And should it be the same for all levels? As a high school umpire, should the width of your zone be what is exactly written in the rulebook? Should it be what the MLB umpires call? Should you go an inch (or so) wider than what is acceptable in MLB?

Assuming the ball meets the height requirements (which will be discussed next), where does it have to be in relation to the plate? Does the entire ball have to cross over the plate? Does it matter if the batter is standing way forward or way back in his batter's box?

To get those answers, you have to dig back into the rules. And again, although there are similar answers to the question, each book says it differently:

NFHS: A strike is charged to the batter when a pitch enters any part of the strike zone in flight and is not struck at.

NCAA: A strike is a legal pitch that enters the strike zone in flight and is not struck at. … Any part of the ball passing over any part of the plate.

PRO: A strike is a legal pitch when so called by the umpire, which is not struck at, if any part of the ball passes through any part of the strike zone.

With the rule in mind, let's determine the width of the strike zone. Under all rules, from the smallest youth ball through the major leagues, the plate is 17 inches wide along the front edge, so that's the starting point for determining the strike zone's width.

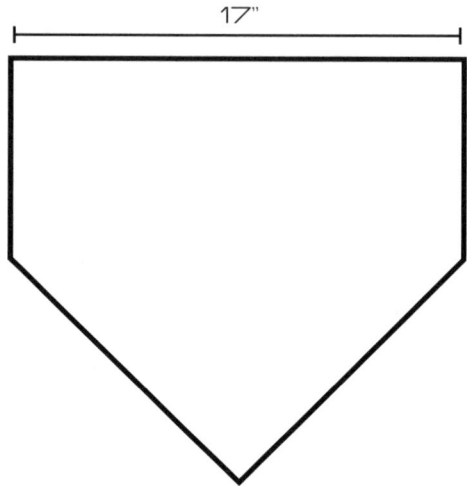

17"

However, that's far from the end of the discussion. As the rules state, any part of the ball passing through any part of the zone is a strike. A baseball is anywhere between nine and 9.25 inches in circumference. That makes the diameter (or width) of a baseball 2.94 inches across. So if any part of that ball touches any part of the plate, it's a strike. That means a tangent strike — where the absolute edge of the ball touches the absolute edge of the plate — is as wide as it can get. Add 2.94 inches to either side of the plate — for a total of 22.88 inches — and you have the actual rulebook strike zone.

When umpires refer to calling a pitch "a ball off the plate," in effect what they are calling is that tangent strike, or the full width of the rulebook strike zone. A ball off the plate is actually another full ball width. While some umpires may consider that too wide of a strike zone, it's actually very close to what is permitted at the highest levels of the game.

> **WHAT TO WATCH:**
> See the width of the strike zone brought to life with examples of pitches on the corner and get a better understanding of the margins of the strike zone.

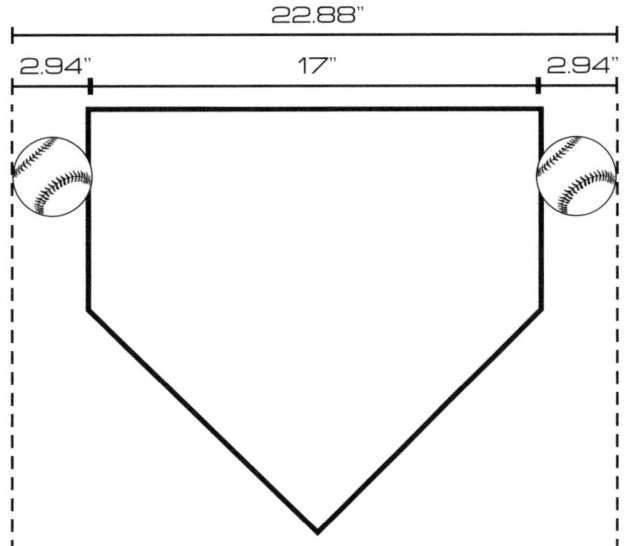

MLB umpires are graded on every pitch that is called (not hit or swung at) during a game. Through a system of cameras and computer software, the position of every pitch is recorded 20 times before it reaches the plate. The pitch is then judged to be a ball or strike and that is compared to the umpire's call.

Because of a variety of factors that a computer cannot determine — the umpire's view being blocked out, the catcher receiving the ball poorly, a tremendous break on a pitch that makes a by-the-letter-of-the-law strike look like a pitch in the dirt — MLB umpires are given a two-inch "buffer" zone in which pitches that are two inches inside or outside that are called strikes are ruled "acceptable" and not incorrect. Those pitches do not count against an umpire's grade.

That gets you to a strike zone of 26.88 inches wide, which is significantly different than the 17-inch wide plate.

Umpire lore has been that an excessively large strike zone is "from batter's box to batter's box." On a properly drawn field, the distance from the inside edge of one batter's box to the other is 29 inches. That is a difference of only 2.12 inches, or just more than one inch wider than what is considered acceptable in MLB.

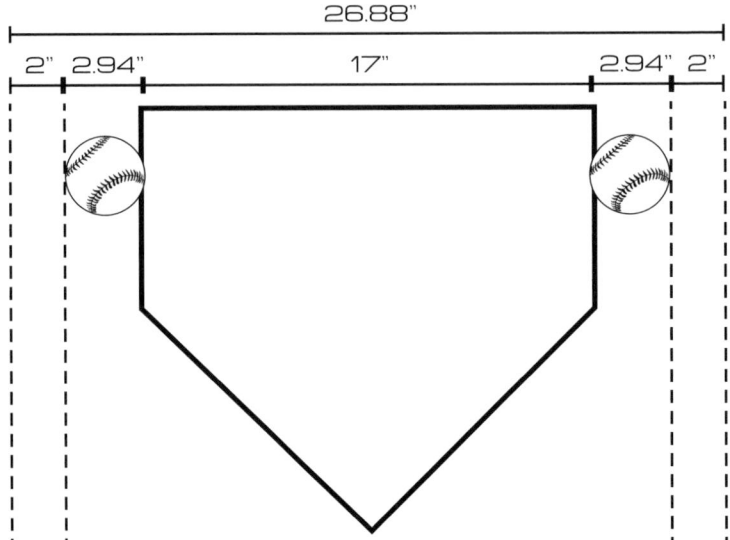

If you asked the average coach, player, fan or umpire if your zone should be an inch bigger on each side than what is called in an MLB game, you would probably get a unanimous "yes" response. Yet if you asked the same people if your strike zone should be from "batter's box to batter's box," those people would likely change their response.

Height of the Zone

Now, let's take a closer look at the definitions in the differences of the wording for the top and bottom of the strike zones.

The definitions also differ in relation to when the pitch is supposed to be judged. In NFHS, the determining factor is the batter's normal stance. However, in the other two codes, it is when he is prepared to swing at the ball. That is believed to mean when he has taken his stride — the instant before swinging.

"It's not clearly laid out in the rulebook," said Justin Klemm, the executive director for the Professional Baseball Umpires Corp. (PBUC), the affiliate of Minor League Baseball (MiLB) that oversees more than 240 umpires. "In my personal approach, it's impossible to define when each batter is prepared to strike at the pitch. That is a concept that is left to the judgment of the umpire.

TOP OF THE ZONE

NFHS	Halfway between the batter's shoulders and the waistline.
NCAA	Midpoint between the top of the shoulders and the top of the uniform pants.
PRO	Horizontal lines at the midpoint between the top of the shoulders and the top of the uniform pants.

BOTTOM OF THE ZONE

NFHS	The knees.
NCAA	Bottom of the kneecaps.
PRO	A line at the hollow beneath the kneecap.

"Did I believe he was in a position just before swinging to hit the pitch? Do I believe he was merely stepping? MLB did a study about 12 years ago. Each batter consistently puts himself into a natural position to strike at the pitch and that's generally that half-step forward.

"The umpire has to visualize that position. If the batter squares to bunt or if the batter just stands there without any movement, the umpire has to set the parameters of the zone depending on where the batter would be if he were in position to strike at the pitch."

WHAT TO WATCH
So what do definitions mean when it comes to the height of the strike zone — both the top and bottom borders of the zone? And what are a couple of techniques that an umpire can use to help judge the height of a pitch?

Understanding the Zone

Do umpires truly understand what constitutes a pitch being in the strike zone?

If you ask the director of umpire training for the NCAA, he likes what he sees when it comes to calling balls and strikes at the college level.

"There are so many eyes on umpires with evaluators traveling to games and the rise of television in the college game," said Tom Hiler, who was also a professional and college umpire for nearly 20 years. "Our umpire clinics stress calling the entire strike zone. I don't buy into the theory that umpires call too many or not enough. Umpires make mistakes on pitches just like anyone at any level. I don't think there's a problem. Do they make mistakes? Yes, but everyone does."

He believes that through the clinics and training that the understanding is much better.

"I think there's a lot more attention to what is a strike and what isn't," Hiler said. "It's not a vague point as it used to be. There's a lot more teaching, instruction and video."

Hiler also attributes the improved zones at the lower level to the changes in MLB.

Starting in 1999, MLB added an electronic system (called QuesTec) that measured the location of pitches in relation to a batter's individual strike zone through the use of multiple cameras. In recent years, MLB has gone to the Z/E system (Zone Evaluation), a more enhanced method for pitch tracking and umpire evaluation.

"One of the things that better defined the strike zone for umpires is when MLB when to the Questec," he said. "There use to be a lot of unwritten rules. MLB had a huge emphasis of eliminating external factors, such as the catcher setting up inside and the ball coming outside. With that type of lead happening at the highest level, it opened our eyes to what we can call."

The Borderline Strikes

The pitch that comes right down the middle is easy to call. For that matter, so is the one that hits the dirt or goes behind the batter. But what about the ones that aren't so easy? Or the ones that are technically strikes, but aren't called consistently?

Probably no pitch has been more debated and discussed than the high pitch — the one that comes over a couple of inches above the belt. That is clearly within the rulebook definition of the strike zone, but is probably the least called pitch of all.

"I think the average umpire certainly knows what the rulebook says about the strike zone," said Mark Uyl, a college umpire who has worked seven NCAA postseason tournaments and is also in charge of baseball umpires for the Michigan High School Athletic Association. "But a lot of times, the average umpire falls into what the game participants accept. As long as coaches aren't screaming, they call what is accepted.

"I really think our interpretation of the top of the strike zone is in error. We all sit at home and watch MLB and anything that's a flyspeck above the belt is called a ball."

Klemm says the reason for the high strike not being called in previous generations, but starting to be called more today, deals with how umpires set up.

"Umpires stand differently behind the plate today," Klemm said. "Umpires are more conscious about how and where they stand. None of that happened in the early stages of baseball. It's been refined by the work of the umpires and the scrutiny of the media.

"Fundamentally, the stances were brutal. There wasn't consistency. Umpires were over the catcher's head. Umpires were moving. Umpire training programs really got started in the 1960s and you are seeing the benefits now."

That still doesn't mean umpires are getting the marginal pitches for strikes often enough.

"Some of the best advice I got when I was moving up in the minor leagues was that if I wanted to be a good umpire, I had to call the inside corner," said retired professional and college umpire David Riley, who is now the chief instructor for the Mike Walsh Memorial Umpire Clinic in Indianapolis. "The person who told me that said, 'That's where you get outs.

That's where you break bats. The guys in his leagues called that corner. Guys want to pitch in there, give them the benefit of the doubt.'"

Riley also said the high strike is getting called more often, but agreed with Uyl on what is accepted is what gets called.

"Guys don't get the high strike because they are conditioned from what they see on TV. It took a long time for MLB to say umpires need to get that high strike."

So What is a Strike?

After all of the definitions and trying to understand what a strike is or is not, you can be reminded about what U.S. Supreme Court Justice Potter Stewart said more than 45 years ago: "I shall not today attempt further to define the kinds of material I understand to be embraced … But I know it when I see it …"

Keep in mind however, he was talking about obscenity, not pitching.

But it's not just a matter of taking one look at one pitch. Determining what is a strike takes a lot of practice, Klemm said.

"The first-year professional player doesn't know the strike zone; neither does a first-year professional umpire," Klemm said. "Umpires have to see enough pitches at the level they are working to know the difference between two close pitches."

Mike Droll, an NCAA umpire for 30 years who has worked 11 NCAA Regionals, said that we don't trust ourselves enough when we do see a pitch that should be called a strike.

"Sometimes, especially with younger umpires or umpires who are moving up to a new level or are working their first big game, they get hesitant to call strikes," Droll said. "It's almost like they are a little bit fearful; they are afraid to look foolish. If they are working their first big series, and they haven't been around long and they want to impress, they tend to be too hesitant to call marginal strikes."

Uyl said he's seen the same thing as well.

"We can definitely call more strikes," he said. "If the level of play gets better and umpires get into big games or tournament games, they get too fine or try to prove how good their eyes really are, leaving strikes on the table."

Riley said not calling enough strikes is a major problem.

"I think some guys are too set on the strike zone without understanding it," he said. "I think a lot of high school umpires are rulebook umpires instead of situational umpires and that's a killer."

What Riley means is you must be aware of the level of game you are working. He doesn't advocate being as tight in youth ball as he was in pro ball. But he retained the same structure of his zone when he retired from the pros and entered the college ranks.

"Everyone said when I went from Triple-A to college ball, I was going to have a tough time," he said. "I didn't change my strike zone one bit. Very seldom did people get upset when I called an aggressive zone."

You can get too big, however. "Guys tend to get wild with their zone sometimes," Droll said. "As umpires get more experienced, they'll think they have the credibility to call that pitch a couple of balls out that is right at the waist."

Is It "Your" Strike Zone?

It would be great if every umpire could go out and judge a game the same way — that no matter who the plate umpire was that day, he would have no different decisions than any other umpire.

Unfortunately, that's not possible. Plate umpires are human beings and not robots.

Even with the strict definitions of what determines a strike, each plate umpire will see and process pitches differently. That will occur from umpire to umpire and even from game to game with an individual umpire.

However, the best umpires will become consistent in what they call. MLB pitcher Roger Clemens famously kept scouting reports on the plate umpires who worked his games. He knew the tendencies of each umpire and used that information to his advantage. The trend of scouting umpires has become standard at the MLB level and has crept into the higher ranks of the college game.

Umpires should strive to call the strike zone as it is written, but know they may not see pitches the exact same way as other umpires.

But do yourself a favor: Get the word "my" out of your strike zone vocabulary. Despite the obvious room for judgment in interpreting the strike zone, the days of "your" strike zone are gone. It is the game's strike zone, as defined by the rulebook, the administrators, the coaches, the players and the umpires. Calling it "your" or "my" strike zone gives the impression that you get to do whatever you want with it, regardless of all those other factors. It has become hot-button phrasing for most coaches and administrators and is best left in history books.

Developing consistency within the rules and finding what works for you and the level of game you are working are what turns the science of the strike zone into the art form. That is what separates the best umpires from the middle of the pack.

Chapter 2
BASIC STANCES

I rish statesman Edmund Burke famously said: "Those who don't know history are destined to repeat it."

While that statement doesn't literally apply to working the plate in a baseball game, there is a lot of truth in it.

To figure out the proper positioning behind the plate and the best stance to use, it's important to take a look at where and how umpires stood in the early days of baseball and how and why it evolved to where it is today.

In the early days of baseball, from the time when umpires first moved behind the catcher until around the 1960s, there was no formal training, so umpires did what they thought gave them the best look.

The balloon or outside protector provided plenty of safety for the umpire's body, but necessitated umpires putting themselves in a bad position to call pitches; being right over the catcher's head made it particularly tough to be consistent on the low pitch.

Over time, through formal and informal umpire schools and training, there is now much better knowledge and of what positioning is best for plate umpires.

Proper Position

The most important thing for a plate umpire is to have his head in the correct position.

The "slot" is thought to be the best overall position to see the entire strike zone. But what exactly is the slot? Simply put, the slot is putting yourself in position between the batter and the catcher. The best position is one in which you line your head up over the inside corner of the strike zone.

The next part of the correct position is having the proper head height. The basic starting position for your head is to have your chin at the top of the catcher's helmet. Once you have advanced to high school and college age players, that will do two things — one, it will enable you to see the entire strike zone (the catcher's head will not block your view of the low and outside pitch) and two, it will put your head at the top of the strike zone.

To review, if your head is correctly in the slot position, you have half of the margins of the strike zone covered. On a right-handed hitter, if the pitch moves your eyes to the left, it's a ball (inside) and if it is above eye level, it's also a ball (high). That simplifies half the decision-making process.

"I'm a big proponent of an umpire putting his inside eye (closest to the catcher) on the black," Riley said. "The plate isn't going to move. Drifting with the catcher causes you to change your strike zone. If I can keep my head in that position, I get the same look at a pitch every time."

Unfortunately, there are plenty of times when circumstances will prevent you from getting your head into the ideal position. The most common situation is the catcher moving inside to receive an inside pitch. Related to that is the batter leaning over the plate in his normal stance.

When your vision is blocked, you must move to see the pitch. The correct way to move is either to get higher or more inside.

If you move lower, the catcher's helmet will block you from seeing the entire strike zone. If you move over the catcher's head or to his outside shoulder, you are putting yourself in harm's way. When the batter fouls a ball off, it is usually directly back. And when you are over the heart of the plate (which is where the catcher's outside shoulder will be when he moves in), you are directly in the line of fire.

In addition, dramatic moves to the outside shoulder completely change your view of the strike zone. A slight move up or in does not affect your perception of the zone, but a drastic move completely affects your perception.

It is important to note that throughout the discussion of the proper position behind the plate, the entire focus to this point has been on the location of your head.

WHAT TO WATCH

It's not about the stance at this point, it's about putting your head (and therefore your eyes) in the correct position. So what does it look like? And what does the problem of being too low look like? And why is it an issue?

That's because in order to get balls and strikes correct, that's the most important factor. It doesn't matter how you stand, as long as your head is in the correct position.

So which stance should you use? MLB umpire Marvin Hudson answered that question in a *Referee* interview in 2004. "Whichever stance feels the most comfortable," he said. "If you are comfortable, then you will be more focused on the game."

Hiler agreed that which stance you pick shouldn't affect your zone.

"It's about putting your head in the best possible position to see pitches," he said. "If you are in the ideal position, it doesn't matter. Your head should be in the same position in whatever stance. Umpires have different feelings with what they need to do with their body and how their body works."

So let's take a look at four of the most common stances. With each of the stances listed, it is assumed that you are getting into position for a right-handed hitter.

The Box

The stance that is taught as the most basic and is the starting point for most umpires is the box stance. Your feet are spread slightly more than shoulder width apart and are placed in a heel-toe configuration, with your left foot slightly ahead of your back foot and your weight evenly distributed on the balls of your feet. While your feet are slightly askew, your body should be square to the pitcher's mound. You should be about four to six inches behind the catcher's heel, far enough to not get in his way and close enough so that your view of the outside corner — you should be able to see well into the opposite batter's box — is not affected.

As the pitcher prepares to deliver the ball, bend at the knees (not the back) as if you were going to sit in a chair. You should have a slight lean forward so that your head gets into the slot position. It is important that your lean is a torso lean and not a back bend. Bending at your back will not be able to put you in the same position over the course of an entire game.

Your right hand should be on your right knee, locked in for support. It's behind the catcher, so you aren't exposed to

BOX STANCE — FRONT VIEW

injury there. However, you must tuck your left hand. The most basic is to rest your elbow on your thigh, leaving your hand loose and behind the catcher. With the left hand being slightly exposed, you don't want it locked (or even against your body, necessarily) since a wild pitch or a foul ball could hit that hand.

"We start with the heel-toe box because it's a known fundamental," Klemm said. "Through trial and error, it's the stance at its most basic level. Umpires are able to get square to the pitcher, get into the slot and maintain proper distance to the catcher."

When he's working with beginning umpires, the box stance is where Riley starts as well.

"It allows for more consistency of head height," Riley said. "Minor adjustments are easier to make from that stance. You

BOX STANCE — SIDE VIEW

just have to go up and down instead of forward and back. One of the things that is key is distance from the catcher. You can be more consistent from the box."

The Scissors

The scissors stance is almost better described as a modified splits stance, because your legs are in a splits configuration, with your left leg in a similar position as in the box stance, but your right leg is directly behind you, acting more like a kick stand, providing balance but not bearing much weight.

As the pitcher delivers, your left leg is bent and your right leg is completely straight. It is important that you do not bend too far forward, because you will then have to crane your neck in order to be looking at the pitch.

Since starting umpiring, Uyl has always worked the scissors and believes there are three big advantages to working that stance.

"It's the most stable position that there is, when you lock in, it's difficult to be sliding up or down," he said. "It also eliminates a lot of the drifting that umpires do in the box. You have a more consistent head position. From game to game, I'm able to get my head in the same spot more than guys who work the box.

SCISSORS — FRONT VIEW

SCISSORS — SIDE VIEW

"Last, you are able to get up into the slot farther; you are able to get your head further forward. The more you can get into the slot, the better look you will get at the pitch that is down and away. We are able to work to see by the catcher, don't have to look through the catcher's head like guys in the box do."

A problem that occurs with the umpire being in the scissors is the position isn't one that is considered athletic.

"You can't do an athletic movement on one leg," Klemm said. "Linebackers don't start in a scissors position."

Another issue with the scissors stance is there is no truly safe place to put your hands. A lot of umpires will rest them at the top of their left thigh, but both hands are at risk. Placing them behind your body disrupts your balance and puts more pressure on your left leg.

Umpires who have worked the scissors in professional baseball have had a tendency to develop lower back and knee problems, some of which have contributed to career-ending injuries.

"I haven't given any thought to changing up. It's a minor concern," Uyl said. "The biggest concern at my level is the frequency. An MLB umpire is working 30-plus plate jobs per year. A minor league umpire is working 40-70 plate jobs per year. In a college season, I'm working 15-16 plate jobs per year. The frequency and opportunities are less."

The Knee

If you are in a proper scissors stance, you are basically in the beginning position for the knee stance. The left leg is in the same position to start, but instead of remaining in a standing position, you drop to one knee.

The knee provides good balance and excellent stability since you aren't moving at all; however, that also can be a disadvantage if either the catcher or hitter makes a late adjustment.

Additionally, with all the movement that is required by the plate umpire, the umpire will spend a lot of time getting up and getting back down.

In a 2008 interview with *Referee*, MLB umpire Wally Bell talked about the most difficult aspect of working the knee.

"The older I get, the harder it is to get the body to work," he said. "Bending down or squatting is hard too, but that's probably one of the reasons guys have gotten off their knee. It just gets so hard. As much as you may move and rotate in the two-umpire system, you still have to move in the four-man system. I have to move on a ground ball to the 45-foot line and

WHAT TO WATCH
The box? The scissors? The knee? Hands-on-knees? Something in between? Before you can figure out which stance works best for you, watch umpires working the various stances in games. We'll point out the things umpires do right and the minor flaws that can affect your stance.

THE KNEE — FRONT VIEW

I have to be able rotate to third base. We are moving on every play."

Droll started out working the scissors, but because of his height (6-foot-4), he was encouraged to try the knee.

"At the time, I was still doubling between part-time Division I and part-time Division III and high school games in the summer," Droll said. "I took some fall games in the late 1990s, experimented with it and fell in love with it right away.

"I've got a consistent position with my head and I don't have to worry about being tired and having my head height start to drop. With replacing pants, it's cost me a lot more money. But it's worth it."

PlayPic®

THE KNEE — SIDE VIEW

Because he must get up and down between every pitch, Droll spends a lot of time working in the gym.

"It's hard on the body, on the core, getting up and down from the knee and being active," he said. "I've always stayed in good shape, but now I work on core exercises religiously — strengthening my glutes, abs and chest."

Working the knee can reduce your presence on the field, but Droll said that it shouldn't be an issue if the knee is worked correctly.

"You are down there to call a pitch and you are back up again," he said. "It's critical to be up and down. You have to work harder to show people you are hustling. The rest of the time you are up, mobile and getting in to position. You don't ever want to give that impression that you are lazy."

One impression he can't avoid is that of unkempt plate pants.

"It looks tacky with dirt on your slacks when you are working," he said. "It diminishes from your appearance, but I don't know how you avoid that."

The Hands-on-Knees

A stance that has gained popularity is the hands-on-knees stance, or the Gerry Davis stance, named after the umpire who popularized it at the MLB level.

The umpire stands about six to 12 inches behind the catcher with the feet square (not in heel-toe) facing the pitcher. As the pitcher delivers, bend more at the knees than at the back and lock in.

The hands-on-knees stance provides the best stability since you are completely locked in and are able to ensure consistent head height throughout the game.

PlayPic®

HANDS-ON-KNEES — FRONT VIEW

HANDS-ON-KNEES — SIDE VIEW

The downside of the hands-on-knees stance is that being further behind the catcher, you run the risk of not being able to see the low or outside pitch. Also because of your position, you are more at risk of being hit by a foul ball or wild pitch.

"It helps umpires who have problems with upper body movement," Klemm said. "It assists umpires who have problem with finding proper torso lean. But it's a safety net. We encourage umpires to not work it. You should be able to grasp the concept of head height, torso lean and sitting into your stance for seven, nine or more innings."

There is also an exposure danger. Umpires who lock their hands on their knees are more susceptible to injury. If their hand is locked in and gets hit, there is nowhere for it to move and with so many small bones unable to take impact, the likelihood of injury is greater.

When to Get into Your Stance

In going through most of the stances, you should have noticed there are two key times in each stance — the position of your feet to get ready and then the final position to be in to see the pitch.

Ideally, you will be in a comfortable position while the players are going through their preliminary motions. You cannot lock in early because you will not be able to hold that position throughout the time the pitcher gets set and delivers the pitch. Additionally, catchers, especially at higher levels, make a late shift outside of the batter's view to provide a target for the pitcher. If you set up too early, you run the risk of having the catcher's adjustment negatively affect your view.

Knowing when to get into your stance "is the most basic fundamental I teach," Hiler said. "Your body is a tripod and your head is the camera. You want to be able to track with your eyes through the strike zone.

"Just as the pitcher gets ready to deliver, you have to have your tripod ready and your camera still to take the picture."

Being set doesn't mean being inflexible.

"At times umpires get into that perfect position and then the catcher makes a secondary adjustment," Hiler said. "The umpire must make adjustments then also. You have to make sure and allow for the catcher to make his adjustment. As the pitcher gets ready, the catcher sets up down the middle; when the pitcher delivers, the catcher will move because the batter is no longer looking at him."

There will be times when you are setting later than is ideal. With experience, you'll be able to deal with that scenario.

"You have to be set as the ball is approaching the zone," Hiler said. "If you are moving while the pitch is coming across the plate, you aren't able to track the ball well. The bottom line

---

WHAT TO WATCH

It's important to get set at just the right time. When you are too late, it causes problems. When you set too early, you lock yourself into a potentially bad spot. Take a look as we point out what's right and what's wrong.

is you have to be set before the ball enters the zone. It's a split-second difference."

One adjustment you should not make is to move too far with the catcher, especially if his adjustment is way outside. You must maintain the same view of the strike zone from the slot position. Even if the pitcher is not trying to throw a strike, giving yourself a different angle to view a pitch can affect future pitch decisions. You want to maintain as consistent position as you can from the first pitch through the final pitch of the game.

At the umpire schools, you will hear the mantra: "On the rubber; get set; call it!" When the pitcher gets on the rubber and takes his sign, prepare to assume your stance and as he begins his windup or comes to a stop in his set position, get in your final stance.

When to Come Out of Your Stance

The simple answer is to come out of your stance after the pitch has been caught, but it's not truly as simple as that. Yes, you have to wait until the end of the pitch in order to judge the pitch, but as you will learn later, there are different times to come out of your stance depending on whether the pitch is a ball or strike.

When you do come out of your stance, come out in the same manner as you went into it — with a smooth, fluid motion.

WHAT TO WATCH

We aren't robots. And over time, flaws will creep into our game. Some of the mistakes that umpires make are obvious; others are more subtle. Take a look at some of the most common flaws and how to avoid them.

Common Themes and Flaws

Head height and positioning are the most important parts of your stance, but there are several other things that should resonate, no matter which stance you select.

Lack of stability. The ability to get into your stance at the correct time and remain still throughout the pitch from the first inning through the last is critical for success as a plate umpire.

That's why finding a good place to put your hands is critical in your stance. By putting your hands or arms in the prescribed position, you have provided extra stability. Regardless of which stance you are in, your back should be straight and you should have very little forward lean. That will make a big difference in your perspective as you see the pitch. When you bend more at the back, you will have to extend your neck. As you get tired in the later innings, you will not be able to maintain the same position and that will affect your zone.

Not getting locked in. If you aren't locked in and in a consistent position, you will not be able to judge pitches the same way every time. That's why you want to be balanced and locked in before every pitch. An umpire who "hides" his hands behind him in an effort to protect them is rarely stable or consistent. Another bad spot for the hands is on the catcher. There are some umpires — mostly those who work the box stance — who will tend to put one hand on the catcher, as a guide for maintaining the proper distance. Putting anything more than the lightest possible touch on the catcher can affect his ability to play. Additionally, not having your hand as a locking mechanism as part of your stance will reduce your stability.

Protection. Protection issues are another common theme. You will get hit by wild pitches and foul balls while working the plate; if you were never going to get hit, you wouldn't need to wear any protective gear. However, you reduce the risk by being in the correct position. Your shinguards will do you no good if your leg is turned so that a loose pitch can hit your leg. If you are locked in throughout the pitch, your protective gear will work best. And if you aren't locked in, you will be more likely to move when that pitch hits the dirt. An umpire who bails out on pitches will end up moving around too much to remain consistent.

Nervousness. It's easy to spot a nervous umpire; he fiddles with the indicator or flails his arms around in between pitches. It's almost like he'd rather be anywhere than behind the plate.

Some umpires seem to get wound up in knots as they prepare to call pitches. Their muscles are tense and they move around way too much. Some have nervous mannerisms that create the perception that they are inexperienced or scared. They may fiddle endlessly with the indicator or look at it after every pitch, paw at the dirt or shift constantly from one foot to the other; they generally look as if they'd rather be somewhere else.

Contrast that with the top umpires — they always look relaxed and in control with no wasted movements. They do not bounce into their stance but settle in and make the difficult job of calling balls and strikes look effortless.

Several flaws tend to be more common in the scissors stance, but can still creep into your game, regardless of which stance you work.

Get squared up. It is imperative to be square to the plate and pitcher. When umpires lose that alignment, their perspective of the corner pitches is affected. It is a bigger problem for umpires who work the scissors since they are putting all of their weight on one leg. Umpires who are relaying on both legs tend to remain more square to the plate.

Get set at the right time. A final flaw is getting set too early. If you do that, by the time the pitch arrives, you are ready to get out of your stance. That will affect your timing — whether it is moving your head with the pitch or not following the ball all the way into the mitt because you are wanting to move. If you come out of the stance too early, your consistency and concentration are ruined.

Chapter 3
THE PITCH

N ear the end of Chapter 1 was the quote from Justice Stewart about knowing it when he saw it. So to know it's a strike, you have to see it. The question for umpires is how do you see a pitch?

Remember, it's a baseball, starting from the pitcher's hand and traveling in less than half a second directly, but not in a straight line, to the catcher's mitt, discounting the ones that bounce or that he misses, which happens all too often at the lower level. And if that weren't tough enough, add in that the pitcher could deliver from his right or left hand and could throw from a variety of positions — over the top, three-quarter, sidearm or submarine.

So how do you go about the task at hand, judging whether the pitch that was just thrown was a strike? There are three things you must do correctly — you must track the pitch, you must show good timing and you must develop good judgment.

Tracking a Pitch

To properly call a pitch, you must track it. You cannot focus on the strike zone or catcher's mitt and wait for the ball to enter that area. You must watch it the entire way from the pitcher's hand, to as one of our experts said, "the back of the catcher's mitt."

Additionally, you must watch the ball with your eyes, and not move your head as the pitch comes in.

"It's the hardest skill to learn in umpiring," said Uyl. "We talk about following the ball and we talk about what the zone is.

"You have to remember the zone is that area out over the plate. There is such a focus to that area and that last six feet from when it's right in front of the plate all the way into the glove."

To follow the ball all the way with your eyes requires discipline and training, and Riley has found that it is easier to teach someone to do that who is new.

"The guys who do it well are the ones who have never umpired before," said Riley. "The toughest is when you have guys who have umpired without much instruction and they've umpired and then get instruction."

Once you have picked up bad habits, they are "very hard to break," Riley added.

So what is the right way to learn?

Riley said the easiest way to get an umpire to track a baseball is to do a practice drill in which someone holds a baseball four or five feet in front of him.

"Have the person holding the ball move it around and your job is to follow it with your eyes," he said. "They get immediate feedback if they are doing it right."

If an umpire is not tracking the ball, but instead is watching the area in front of the plate, the appearance of the ball will cause him to blink. That split second of barely seeing the ball, blinking and trying to pick up the ball again will result in a very inconsistent manner of calling pitches.

"You can't just stare straight ahead," said Klemm. "That tends to promote tunnel vision."

It is imperative to track the pitch with only the eyes, and not with head movement, according to Klemm.

"Head movement is a poor habit and something that umpires must stay away from," he said. "When you allow that to sneak into your work, it will cause some inconsistency. As you become more comfortable, the head movement increases and it doesn't become conscious to stay still."

Once umpires have advanced to higher levels and seen many pitches, some natural head movement may happen.

"You still have to start with no head movement, but you have to allow for natural movement," Klemm said "We may allow natural head movement depending on the location of the pitch. I think when our guys go to the higher levels and they are getting the pitch right, it's less of an issue. At the lower levels, if you are moving your head, you are going to have problems."

WHAT TO WATCH

So what does tracking a pitch look like? It enables the plate umpire to see the pitch all the way into the mitt and get the call correct. The video shows the several pitches the umpire tracked all the way into the mitt and what it looks like when an umpire follows the ball with his head and not his eyes.

Timing

Tracking a pitch and timing go hand-in-hand. When most non-umpires get asked about timing, they think of speed — how fast something is accomplished. Timing when it comes to calling a pitch is being deliberate, seeing the entire pitch and only then rendering a judgment.

For those of you who have ever seen the old slapstick comedy, *The Naked Gun* — there is a great example in that movie about timing. When the police detective impersonates the plate umpire, he gives two very poor examples of timing and one pitch with absolute perfect timing.

After the first pitch is thrown, it takes the "umpire" at least four seconds to realize his task, and everyone waits patiently for him to ring up a pitch that split the strike zone in all directions.

The second pitch is called with excellent timing. He follows the ball into the glove, takes a moment to process what he saw and comes up with the decision.

Unfortunately, it didn't last. On the third pitch of the sequence, he's calling the batter out on strike three and going into a moonwalk before the pitch reaches the plate. (To see the video, do a YouTube search for "Leslie Nielsen umpire.")

Before we talk about the good aspects of timing, let's review why the first pitch is not good timing. There are several bad techniques or theories when it comes to timing.

One is to listen for the sound of the glove, wait a prescribed amount of time and then make the call. Another is the whisper technique. Wait for the pitch, listen to the ball hit the mitt, whisper to yourself, "That pitch was a strike (or ball)," and then make the call.

To make it clear, timing is not waiting longer to announce your decision; if that is what you are doing, you are just waiting longer to make a bad decision because you judged the pitch too soon.

So what is good timing?

"Proper use of eyes," said Klemm. "When I know my timing is dead on, it's because of proper use of eyes. See the pitch, see the pitch, see the pitch. When I've done that, I've never had to worry about timing. If I properly see the pitch, my mind will register what word needs to come out of my mouth and what my arm and body need to do.

"Don't think about the pitch, just watch it. Turn to me and tell me what it was. That's timing."

And another expert takes watching the pitch a step farther.

"You have to follow the ball into the back of the mitt, instead of just the mitt," Riley said. "If you are looking at the back of his hand, you know you saw it all the way in. The better you are tracking, the better your timing. You are seeing it all the way. When you are really fast, you aren't tracking the ball."

WHAT TO WATCH

If you can develop good timing, you'll become a much better umpire. Take a look at what good timing looks like on several pitches.

Into the Mitt

Imagine having to decide if a pitch was a strike without having the catcher there to stop it. Of course, that would be painful since it would probably hit you, but the point should be clear.

By the time the ball is into the mitt, it has passed through the strike zone. If you believe people who have never umpired, the ball being caught shouldn't matter.

Not only is it critical for timing, as previously explained in this chapter, but it provides a final frame of reference for judging the pitch itself.

When and how the catcher receives the ball matters. Especially from the dugout, team personnel can't see whether the ball was inside, outside or in the zone. But they can all tell whether a ball was too high or too low just by looking at where the ball was caught.

Think about a looping curve ball that just catches the bottom of the zone at the front of the plate. By the time it travels the remaining three or four feet to the catcher's glove, he's scooping it off the ground. While by rule, it might have been a true strike, it's almost impossible to call because of how it was caught.

The best catchers work to receive the ball and present a view of the pitch to the umpire without a lot of movement — both before the pitch arrives and moving the glove as he catches the pitch.

A catcher will take close pitches and present them to the umpire in the best way possible. That is called framing.

Umpiring would be a lot easier if catchers didn't move to block the umpire's view. That's why it is important for the umpire to get set only after the catcher has made his final adjustment as was covered in the previous chapter.

The other movement that a catcher has is more subtle. That movement is how he catches the pitch.

Ideally, a catcher would catch a pitch and never move his glove afterward. The umpire would get a perfect view of the pitch's location as it hit his mitt. However, that is a rare occurrence. Most catchers are trying to encourage umpires to call strikes by making the pitch appear as good as possible.

Catchers will do that through two different techniques — framing and yanking (or pulling). When a catcher frames the pitch, he is moving or turning just his glove as or immediately after he receives the pitch. If he moves his arm, he is yanking the pitch.

When done correctly, the catcher frames the pitch. While the glove may be just outside the zone, the ball appears to be a strike, even if it really isn't.

The fact is that framing pitches is a skill that is acquired over a lot of time. That fact has to be considered as a reason why we struggle to call more strikes.

"Why we can't (call more strikes) is because we watch so much baseball on TV and we see the best catchers framing and presenting pitches," Uyl said. "The better our catching, the more aggressive we can be."

What causes problems is when a catcher does more than just frame the pitch. If the catcher receives the pitch and moves the glove back into the strike zone, he is yanking the pitch, which is an action that is trying to deceive the umpire.

Klemm would tell catchers that wasn't helping their cause.

"I would tell them, 'You pulled that back,'" he said. "'The ball was off the plate and you knew it because you pulled it back.'"

Yanking is when a catcher takes a pitch that is outside the strike zone and brings it back, holding it to make it appear it was a strike.

Not every pitch a catcher frames will be a strike, and some that he yanks may not be out of the zone. But you can certainly use the catcher's mitt as a tool to finish off your picture of the strike.

You've set up properly; you've picked up the ball out of the pitcher's hands; you've tracked it all the way to the back of the catcher's mitt; you've seen how and where he caught it. Now it's time to make the call.

WHAT TO WATCH

Catchers will try to convince you to call a pitch is a strike, either by framing it for you to see, or by yanking it back into the zone. What's the difference? Watch umpires call several strikes on pitches that aren't received well.

Chapter 4
MAKING THE CALL

There are many different ways to call the pitch and announce your decision. However, there are some fundamentals that must be followed and some very bad habits that have crept into mechanics over time.

The most important thing for an umpire to do is to judge each pitch on its merits alone.

There are some umpires and instructors who believe the way to calls balls and strikes is to believe a pitch is a strike until it convinces you otherwise.

While that philosophy may help someone who is afraid to call strikes, it's a technique that shouldn't be necessary.

Doing what is prescribed by picking the ball up and following it through the time when it hits the back of the mitt should enable you to make the correct judgment. Don't start off with any preconceived ideas about each pitch. Have a blank slate each time the pitcher toes the rubber.

Called Ball

A ball is possibly the easiest pitch to call, because there is nothing to do other than announce your decision.

Once you have determined the pitch was not a strike and the batter did not swing, a call of "Ball" is all that is required.

You can announce the first part of the count, "Ball one," "Ball two," if you desire, but that is information that can easily be given when you give the count.

One habit that you should definitely avoid is announcing the location — the pitch is either in the strike zone or not.

"Do not map pitches," Riley said. "If they aren't asking, I'm not telling."

The problem with doing that is you are inviting a discussion from the dugout if you say the ball was down and the coach disagrees.

"You are automatically in an argument," he added. "When I ball a pitch, he may not ask, he may not care or he may think it's a ball too."

But when he disagrees, he'll say that he has to have that pitch. "Now you are in an argument," Riley said. "Now what have you done?"

The other problem that comes in calling pitches that are outside the strike zone is calling the obvious pitches too quickly.

"We see guys vary their timing based on the location of the pitch," Klemm said. "If you have quick timing on an obvious ball, you've allowed a bad habit to creep into your game.

"If you allow different sequences into your game, you will get smoked on a close pitch eventually. You have fundamentally done something that is terrible for you. It's imperative that you keep your timing the same."

The other problem that arises is when umpires don't verbalize their call of a pitch.

"You always verbalize," Klemm said. "The loudness should reflect the closeness of the pitch. It's your job to call the pitch, so do it."

Klemm did not advocate "screaming" the call, but a good, hard loud call on a close pitch is just like selling a bang-bang play on the bases.

Called Strikes

Mechanically, called strikes are tougher than called balls, because you now have to integrate body movement with your voice and decision.

Once you have decided the pitch is a strike, again by tracking the ball all the way into the mitt and using good timing to process the decision, you are ready to announce the call.

To call a strike, come out of your stance and coordinate your voice with your mechanic. Both should occur at the same time. You have several choices with your mechanic for the called strike, but you should be consistent on strikes one and two, using the same mechanic for each.

The most basic is the "bang on the door" call that is also used for a routine out. As you rise out of your stance, your right arm comes forward with your hand balled in a fist. The movement is usually fairly quick, as the bang-on-the-door description implies.

Another common called strike mechanic is when the umpire turns to his right and points with one finger. Turning your back to the plate and pointing with your right hand to the left side, which some umpires will do with left-handed batters, is not a good habit because you are turning away from any potential play. And while those potential plays happen very rarely, when they do happen, the umpire cannot use, "I was turned away calling a strike," as a legitimate excuse for missing what happened.

Umpires use many different voices with called strikes. There are umpires who say the word, "Strike," while others will say, "Yes," or "Yep." An additional option is that some umpires will use a guttural grunt without saying an actual word. Finally, some umpires will call the number of the strike, "Strike one," or "Strike two." That is what is taught when umpires first learn to call strikes and becomes optional as umpires advance.

There is less need to vary your voice because there is no difference in a "close strike" and one that is right down the heart of the plate. And as Klemm said, bringing different habits into your calls can result in you altering your timing, which will affect your game at some point.

There are umpires who will call strike while in their stance and then come out of their stance and give their hand motion. That is very confusing for all participants except the hitter and catcher, who are the only ones who typically hear the call.

WHAT TO WATCH

There are many ways an umpire can call and signal a strike. The video explains what's good and why certain techniques are not as good.

Swinging Strikes

A swinging strike is called using the same mechanic as a called strike. The difference is there is no voice necessary.

It is obvious to everyone — offense and defense — when a batter has swung at a pitch. There is no need to make a verbal call. However, it is still important that you acknowledge the swing with your called strike mechanic.

There are umpires who advocate using a different mechanic, to distinguish that the call was for the swing as opposed to the pitch. That is not necessary and complicates your actions. The best advice for an umpire is to keep it simple behind the plate — one basic strike call, with voice on the pitch and without voice if called on the swing, even if it's strike three.

Foul Balls

When the batter makes contact with the baseball, but it doesn't go into fair territory, a strike is normally charged to the count. Where the ball goes and how it gets there determines how the ball is ruled and how the umpire should call it.

A foul ball is defined in the NFHS book as follows:

A foul ball is a batted ball that meets any of the following conditions:

- It settles on foul territory between home and first base or between home and third base.
- It bounds past first or third base on or over foul territory.
- It first falls on foul territory beyond first or third base.
- While on or over foul territory, it touches the person of an umpire or a player or any object foreign to the natural ground.
- It touches the ground after inadvertently being declared foul by an umpire.

The ball becomes dead immediately when a foul ball touches any object other than the ground or any person other than a fielder, goes directly from the bat to the catcher's protector, mask or person without first touching the catcher's glove or hand or becomes an uncaught foul.

A batter is also out when a foul ball (other than a foul tip not a third strike) is caught by a fielder or such catch is prevented by a spectator reaching into the playing area or an attempt to bunt on third strike is a foul.

The NCAA and pro definitions are virtually identical.

When declaring a foul ball, the umpire should use the same emphasis that would be used on a play on the bases. Obvious fall balls — for example, balls hit behind the backstop or well out of the park to either side — need only a slight acknowledgement, if any call at all. Everyone in the park knows the ball was foul, so there is no need to call it.

On the other hand, a ball that is a screamer down the third-base line requires a very definitive call.

The proper mechanic for calling a ball foul is to call time — put both hands up in the air — and then call, "Foul," while pointing to the foul side of the field.

WHAT TO WATCH

All foul tips need to be signaled, but not all foul balls. Take a look at several plays and note the signals that the umpire makes or doesn't make.

A foul ball counts as a strike, except that a batter cannot be out on strikes for hitting a foul ball. The ball is always dead when a ball is determined to be a foul ball.

Foul Tip

A foul tip is a special kind of foul ball. Even though the ball was not hit into fair territory, there are certain conditions that determine if a ball is to be treated as a foul tip and not a foul ball.

For the ball to be a foul tip, it must be a batted ball that goes directly to the catcher's hands and is legally caught by the catcher.

A foul tip is always charged as a strike, even on strike three.

To indicate a foul tip, the plate umpire should slide one hand across the other, visible for all to see and then give the swinging strike mechanic (no voice). The ball remains live and in play on a foul tip.

Checked Swings

While an obvious swing or foul ball is a very simple call and doesn't need any special mechanics, a checked (or half) swing can be imminently more difficult and definitely requires a more set procedure.

Part of the problem with the checked swing is there is only one rules code that clearly defines the moment that an attempt by the batter becomes a strike.

The NCAA defined the half swing as "An attempt by the batter to stop the forward motion of the bat while swinging, which puts the batter in jeopardy of a strike being called. The half swing shall be called a strike if the barrel head of the bat passes the batter's front hip. AR — This does not apply to a bunt attempt when the batter pulls the bat back."

The NFHS book defines a strike as it relates to a swing only as "A strike is charged to the batter when a pitch is struck at and missed (even if the pitch touches the batter)." The pro book, in the definition of a strike, gives virtually the same definition minus the parenthetical.

It is important to note that the batter breaking his wrists, crossing the front of the plate or any other so called "defining points" of when an attempt becomes a swing are not in the rulebooks, but are instead, rooted in folklore and tradition (just as the hands being part of the bat or ties go to the runner).

The first thing to do when there is an attempt by the batter to check his swing is to stick with the pitch itself. And that's not an excuse.

"I'm a firm believer in plate umpires not using that 'they had to watch the pitch as well' as an excuse to not get checked swings right," Klemm said. "You can see both the pitch and the swing. If your timing is proper, you can get them yourself."

When the pitch is a strike without the batter's attempt, there is no need to worry about the swing — call the strike and move to the next pitch.

If the pitch is out of the zone and you judge the batter to have not swung, that is the time to sell the pitch: "Ball, no he didn't go." By doing that, you are taking ownership of the call. It is possible the defense will still appeal, but giving your statement that he did not go will reduce the amount of appeals.

You do not have to be real loud on saying that you don't believe he went. Say it loud enough for the batter and catcher to hear. That way if you appeal to your partner and he has a swing, it creates less conflict.

If the defense (catcher or coach) asks you to appeal to your partner, you are required to do so under pro and college rules. NFHS rules say the plate umpire "may" ask for help, but it is highly recommended that you always do. By not doing so, you are inviting criticism because you are unwilling to get help.

There are times when you would want to appeal before you are asked by the defensive team.

On a close decision with two strikes, the batter will be out if the checked swing attempt is ruled a strike. If an out is possible, you should find out as soon as possible if it is going to be granted.

That situation becomes more urgent if the ball is not caught and the batter has the opportunity to run to first base (with two outs or with first base open and less than two outs). In that case, to give both the offense (batter trying for first) and the defense (attempt to put out the batter or possibly other runners), the appeal should be immediate.

At the MLB level, the appropriate base umpire may rule on the potential third strike before being asked by the plate umpire. That is called the voluntary strike. Even if the appeal is not instant from the plate umpire, the appropriate base umpire may "immediately and voluntarily" make a strike call if the base umpire is going to reverse the "ball" call of the plate umpire. That gives the batter the immediate opportunity to run.

That mechanic is reserved for professional baseball and should not be used at the lower levels.

When you appeal, point with your left hand toward your partner and ask, "Did he go?" You can start with the base umpire's first name to get his attention in case he's focused on other things at the moment you start to ask.

WHAT TO WATCH
A checked swing can be tough for an umpire to call from behind the plate. When he calls it himself, he needs to indicate that he called the swing. And if he appeals, he needs to do it correctly. The video shows the right mechanics to follow.

When asked, the base umpire should render his decision. There are no hidden agendas or secret systems when it comes to checked swing appeals.

"If I thought he went, I'm going to ring it up," Klemm said. "It's the same as, 'See a balk, call a balk.'"

Hiler said appeals are the reason that the NCAA asks base umpires to be focused on the batter's actions.

"Expect a checked swing; you must watch the barrel of the bat," he said. "Base umpires must remain engaged and focused at all times to see that."

If the pitch is out of the zone and you judge the batter to have swung, you will need to indicate that is the reason the batter is being charged a strike. Come out of your stance as if you were calling a strike and point at the batter with your right hand, saying, "Yes, he went." Then complete the swinging strike mechanic.

The reason to point with your right hand is because that is your strike-calling hand. When you appeal on those you don't call, you point with your left hand. You do not want to point at the batter with your left hand, saying that he went, while your partner, thinking you are making an appeal, calls out, "No, he didn't."

> **▶ WHAT TO WATCH**
> The batter shows a bunt. The video shows several bunt attempts and explains why the batter was or was not charged with a strike.

Bunt Attempts

The final type of swinging strike is a bunt attempt. The NCAA's rule on the bat crossing the front hip does not apply, so it comes down to the umpire's judgment on whether the batter offered at the pitch.

For the batter to have offered, he must have moved the bat toward the ball in an attempt to hit it. Unlike in some softball codes (and baseball lore), it is not a strike if the batter holds the bat in the strike zone and fails to remove it.

Treat a bunt attempt like a checked swing; that is, go through the same mechanics when announcing your decision.

When the batter attempts a drag bunt, it can be very difficult to see both the pitch and the batter's attempt, since the batter is also on his way out of the box.

"There are times it's impossible for one of your eyes to go one way and the other to go the other direction," Hiler said. "The key is to get set, slow your timing down and see the whole play.

"When umpires don't do a good job, their timing is quick and they see the pitch and make the decision on the pitch and, 'Oh wow, there was a checked swing.'"

Called Third Strikes

There is probably no more individualism in baseball than when looking at how the plate umpire signals a called third strike. A called third strike is the one time that an umpire is permitted to get excited on a pitch.

And while that is not necessarily bad, a lot of the mechanics that have developed are wrought with poor habits that will show up in your game at bad times.

There are all kinds of types of called third strikes — the chainsaw, the bow and arrow, the punchout are some of the common names.

But when you start interjecting your personal style, Klemm is very aware that he starts to see fundamentals break down.

"The umpire's head starts to turn away from the plate," he said. "It becomes, 'How do I look?' more than, 'Did I get the pitch right?'

"Am I able to call interference or a dropped third strike if my head is turned away? That is a major problem with what people do on dropped third strikes."

Hiler sees a problem not only with the umpires, but with umpire trainers at camps and clinics when it comes to called third strikes.

"I think a lot of younger instructors that are teaching people spend a lot of time instructing on umpiring styles," Hiler said. "There's too much emphasis on style of how you umpire. When you see instructors who have been doing it a long time, those officials have a tendency to concentrate on the finer details on umpiring."

Those traits then carry over to what feedback umpires are seeking.

"Umpires come up to me and ask, 'How did I look? Did you like my mechanics?'" Hiler said. "Unless there's something wrong with it, I don't worry about it. It's all about whether you get the pitch right or wrong. When they become better umpires, they worry about their calls. I don't care how a guy calls a strike; I'm just concerned about getting pitches right."

Klemm agrees that too much emphasis is placed on the style of the call.

"A good third strike call starts with good fundamentals," he said. "It is natural looking. It third doesn't look forced or rehearsed.

"It just flows with your body style. I don't think guys develop their good third strike call until they have worked a few years. It's a eureka moment. In one moment, he finds it and that's his strike three call."

WHAT TO WATCH

There are a lot of ways to signal a called third strike. Some however can create more problems than they are worth. The video shows you right and wrong ways to make that call.

Outlier Pitches

Some pitches, just because of circumstance, are absolutely "no-win" pitches to call. Those pitches are because of the way they are caught, the way the catcher sets up, the game situation or other circumstances.

A common myth is that a catcher must actually catch the pitch for it to be called a strike. Nowhere in the definition of a pitch or a strike does it say the pitch has to be caught. However, naysayers will argue that if the pitch isn't caught, that it wasn't in a place the catcher could catch it so it must have been outside the zone.

"To call any pitch a ball just because the catcher drops the pitch is not appropriate," Hiler said. "For example, if a catcher drops a pitch that is right down the middle of the zone, an umpire should always call the pitch a strike."

What it comes down to is basic. The catcher catching the pitch is the end point of you watching it. Where the glove is and how the ball is caught is definitely a tool, but it is not the deciding factor. If the pitch is clearly a strike, call it. If the pitch was borderline, and the catcher misplayed it, use that information and determine it wasn't in the zone. There are just no hard-and-fast rules.

"I think umpires at times will take how the catcher catches the pitch on those pitches that are extremely borderline in determining whether it is a ball or a strike," Hiler said.

Another example of an outlier pitch is the 0-2 pitch. When the pitcher has a batter in the hole with two strikes, he will typically attempt to "waste" the next pitch — whether it is an attempt to get the batter to swing at a bad pitch or to set up the following pitch. Very rarely is the pitch intended to be thrown as a strike; instead it will usually be aimed high and over the plate or well off the outside corner.

When a catcher sets up way outside, he is indicating to the offensive team (and to the umpire) that his intention is to not have a strike thrown. So even if the pitch is thrown directly to the mitt and the catcher is able to catch it without moving his mitt, the entire world thinks it is going to be a ball.

Regardless of what the participants think, an umpire's job is to call the pitch as it was. In the example above, it is possible that the catcher deceived the offense by not moving as far outside the zone as possible.

Keep in mind, there are plenty of pitchers who will try to paint the corner for the strikeout by catching the batter off guard.

Don't penalize the pitcher on 0-2 or reward him on 3-0 with an expanded zone. Guard against doing what's expected and call the pitch on its merit.

The last example goes hand-in-hand with the previous one. What is an umpire to do when the catcher moves way inside or outside and the pitcher misses the intended spot so bad that the catcher has to lunge for the ball that was grooved right down the middle of the zone?

In the past, that pitch was easy to call. The pitcher didn't hit his intended spot so he wouldn't be rewarded. Besides, the catcher had to lunge for the ball. Nevermind that he lunged his way right back into the strike zone.

But today, with the prevalence of video, that's a much tougher decision.

"Where we currently are in the evolution of umpiring in the game, catching is going to impact it if it's borderline," Uyl said. "The prevalence of video is the issue. In the old days, there was absolutely no doubt of us calling the pitch how the catcher presented it.

"But being in a supervisory role, I get sent a video of that pitch. That's becoming harder and harder to defend. Freshmen and JV games are ending up on YouTube; it's a different scenario than it was 20 years ago."

Penalty Balls and Strikes

There are several instances in the rulebook in which a ball or strike is added to the count without a pitch being thrown or regardless of whether the pitch was thrown. Those instances are very rare; in fact, you may go the majority of your career without calling them. However, it is important to know the rules regarding them and how to indicate that you have enforced a penalty.

The most common penalty "ball" that you would add to the count is if the pitcher goes to his mouth. Under pro rules, the pitcher is not permitted to touch the ball after touching his mouth or lips while on the dirt circle. If the pitcher legally goes to his mouth, he must wipe his hand off before touching the ball.

The pitcher is not allowed to touch his mouth or lips at all while he is in contact with the pitcher's plate. However, prior to the start of the game played in cold weather and with agreement of both managers, it may be permitted for the pitcher to blow on his hand while in contact with the pitcher's plate.

In the NCAA and NFHS, the pitcher may go to his mouth while on the dirt circle, but he must still wipe off his fingers before touching the ball.

If a pitcher violates, the umpire shall call time and indicate that a ball has been added to the count. The umpire typically does that by putting his hand to his mouth and then indicating a ball. The umpire should then show the new count. The umpire should also switch out the baseball because of the violation.

The second most common violation is for the pitcher failing to deliver within the allotted amount of time.

For pro rules, when the bases are unoccupied, the pitcher shall deliver the ball to the batter within 12 seconds after he receives the ball. Each time the pitcher delays the game by violating this rule, the umpire shall call a ball. The 12-second timing starts when the pitcher is in possession of the ball and the batter is in the box, alert to the pitcher. The timing stops when the pitcher releases the ball. The intent of the rule is to avoid unnecessary delays. The umpire shall insist that the catcher return the ball promptly to the pitcher, and that the pitcher take his position on the rubber promptly. Obvious delay by the pitcher should instantly be penalized by the umpire.

For NCAA, the amount of time permitted is 20 seconds and it begins when the pitcher has the ball on the dirt circle. The timing stops when the pitcher begins his pitching motion. Each pitcher is afforded one warning for his first violation of the rule. All subsequent violations by that pitcher result in a ball being added to the count.

In NFHS, the time limit is 20 seconds, but it applies throughout the game, not just when there are no runners on base. The pitcher must do something (pitch, throw to a base or legally feint a throw to a base) in order to avoid the penalty. The only guidance for starting the clock is that umpires are to require that the ball be returned to the pitcher promptly after each pitch or pickoff attempt.

For pro and NCAA, timing the violations is possible because one of the base umpires will have a stopwatch for timing purposes. That is not common in NFHS play, so umpires should use their best judgment and only penalize when it is apparent the rule has been violated.

The third and least common penalty ball is not really a penalty at all; it's just a very low pitch. If the pitcher drops the ball during his delivery and is rolls across the foul line, a ball is added to the count. If the ball is picked up before crossing a foul line, it is no pitch with no runners on base or a balk with a runner or runners on base.

There are also several penalty strikes that can be awarded, one that applies to all codes and one that applies to one rules code only.

In each rule code, there is a list of eight times the batter is permitted to leave the batter's box between pitches. Those times are when he swings at a pitch, when he is forced out of the box by the pitch, when he attempts a drag bunt, when the catcher or pitcher feints or makes a play at any base, the pitcher leaves the dirt circle, time is granted, the catcher does not catch the pitch or when the catcher leaves his box to give signs or adjust equipment. That list from the NFHS is similar (but not identical to) the NCAA and pro rule.

If the batter leaves the box when he is not permitted to do so, the umpire should encourage him to immediately return to the box (see "Working with the Hitter"). If the batter fails to return promptly, a strike shall be charged. If the batter continues to remain outside the box, additional strikes may be charged, but every effort should be made to avoid that circumstance.

Once the batter is in the box and the pitcher is ready to deliver, the NFHS rules offer an additional opportunity for a penalty strike.

If the batter, without being granted time, steps out of the batter's box with one foot and the pitcher legally delivers the pitch, the pitch is a strike (no matter its location) and the ball remains live. If the batter steps out with both feet, the batter shall be charged with one strike for leaving the box and an additional strike if the pitcher delivers (no matter the location of the pitch).

For NCAA and pro rules, the pitch must be delivered and it is called what it is. There is no set penalty on the batter.

The last penalty ball or strike that exists is the NCAA timing rules that started in 2011. In addition to the pitcher having 20 seconds to deliver the ball with no runners on base, the base umpire is responsible for timing 90 seconds between innings (or 108 seconds in a non-internet televised game). That time limit starts when the last defensive player crosses the foul line toward his dugout and ends when the returning pitcher begins his pitching motion to start the next inning. The rule does not apply if a new pitcher is inserted into the game to start the half-inning. If delays by the defense are the reason for the game not starting within the time limit, a ball is added to the count. If the offense is not ready (batter in the box) at the end of the time limit, a strike is added to the count. There are no warnings for the violation.

The NFHS permits a returning pitcher five throws to be completed in one minute from the third out of the previous inning, but that is rarely enforced since umpires are not carrying watches. If penalized, a ball is added to the count. There is no specific timing rule against the batter being ready, but if he fails to enter the box, he may be charged with a strike as described previously.

Pro rules set the limit of eight pitches to be completed within one minute, but do not specify when that minute starts or the penalty if they are not completed within the time limit. A ball is added to the count when a pitcher exceeds the legal amount of throws between innings.

Chapter 5
WORKING
WITH THE
PARTICIPANTS

Y our decisions about balls and strikes, while final, will not come without scrutiny. Every hitter, catcher, pitcher and coach — even though they all say they don't want the job — will criticize the decisions you make.

Part of the reason for that truly has nothing to do with you or the calls. The teams and players are fighting to win every game and are looking for every competitive advantage they can find. It wouldn't matter if you called every pitch correctly, someone will assuredly tell you that you missed a pitch, or two, or three, or … you get the point.

Balls and strikes are calls that participants are prohibited from arguing, but only the most autocratic umpire will prevent all discussion on those decisions. And someone who does that is likely spelling the end of his career advancement as well, since especially at the amateur level, umpires are rated by coaches, and supervisors are usually not re-hiring umpires who are unapproachable and belligerent with coaches and players.

So the question becomes … how much conversation or discussion is appropriate with catchers, hitters, pitchers and coaches? The answers vary on the position of the person talking and the tone of the conversations.

Working With Catchers

Twenty-five years ago, it was very common for plate umpires to carry on lengthy conversations with catchers. By the end of the game, umpires would know what year the catcher was in school, how his grades were, what kind of year he was having and if he hoped to go to play at the next level. There may have been more than a few jokes or improper remarks, and it stayed between the umpire and the catcher.

Today, the game has become more businesslike and times have changed to the point where any conversation that could be considered inappropriate is no longer welcome. The less you say to a player, the less that can be misconstrued. However, you must develop a good working relationship.

"I think the amount that you talk to catchers has certainly decreased," Uyl said. "Coaches want their kids to play; they don't want their kids' attention diverted by banter with the umpire. The more friendly conversations we used to have have come to an end."

About the only time to be "friendly" with the catcher is before the first actual pitch of the game is thrown by each team. The plate umpire should introduce himself to the catcher and then observe four to six warmup pitches on each side. That lets the umpire observe not only how the pitcher throws, but how the catcher receives the ball.

The plate umpire can also "call" the pitches to himself, working on seeing the ball all the way into the mitt and establishing his timing.

Many catchers, especially at higher levels, will tell umpires what type of pitches the pitcher throws. That information may satisfy a curiosity, but the plate umpire will have no way of knowing which pitch is being thrown once the game starts.

And once the game starts, the casual conversation should come to a half.

"When I do have to communicate with a catcher, it's for informational purposes only and for specific reasons or an issue," Uyl said. "If you are working a high school game, you don't need to be making 17- or 18-year-old friends, it's a business conversation, not a social one."

Part of that business conversation — if not all of it — is dealing with whether he agreed with your call on pitches. Remember, in all likelihood, you will be working with him for the complete game when his team is on defense.

"He can't ask you every pitch," Hiler said. "And you can't stand back there and ask him every pitch if you got it right or wrong."

That said, there is nothing wrong with going about it the right way on close pitches. When a catcher reacts, it's probably because he thought you may have missed the pitch. If he says something, it's OK to tell him you will take a closer look the next time. You are not admitting that you missed it, but you are giving him the courtesy and respect that a good working relationship deserves.

You have to be careful how much you talk to a catcher, because everything you say to that catcher will get repeated to his coach. Recall the "telephone" game from your elementary school days and know that what you tell him will not be what he tells his coach.

Hiler suggests dealing directly with coaches.

"At the college level, the colleges prefer you to talk to the coaches rather than with the player," Hiler said. "I caution umpires to not tell the catchers what they need to do. The umpires are better off developing a working relationship with the coaches. The coaches see that as you coaching their kids.

"Anything you can say will be held against you. Less is better. Eliminate the chances of your words getting misunderstood."

Klemm agreed that you can talk to catchers, but you must keep it productive and constructive.

"You aren't there to coach or teach," he said. "At the professional level, you should never ever coach or tell people how they are going to do things. We never tell anyone how to catch."

Even when a catcher isn't doing a very good job, you can't become a coach. Even if you think they are hurting their own team.

"It's a tough call, because you can't coach catchers," Riley said. "If they are taking pitches away, I'll ask them to stick it for me without holding it too long. I want to get strikes.

"If they are just flipping at the ball and not working to get strikes, you can't do much. You have to be careful who you are dealing with because the kid will go right to the coach and rat you out. They're not professionals and they are scared of their coach. They will do whatever their coach says. You have to try to work with them."

In working the knee, Droll has a unique challenge and reason to talk to catchers.

"It can be tough timing when to get down and get set, especially with catchers who don't get set early," he said. "I don't like to talk to catchers, especially casually. But I will tell them I want their pitcher to get every strike they can. So I encourage them to get set as soon as possible. When I go down, I'm not going to move again. But I need to know their position early."

One thing you have to be very careful with is outright saying you missed a pitch.

"By the time what you said gets to the coach, you will have told the catcher that you missed 15 pitches," Hiler said. "I have done it, but you have to be careful with it. It will be held against you."

Uyl is more careful in what he says in relation to a possible miss.

"I will say I had it a little bit inside or down and for them not to be afraid to go back there," Uyl said. "You may have a borderline pitch away. You do want to let them know that you thought it was close, but I don't ever want to let them know I missed one. Saying to go back there again is effective without admission or conveying too much."

One way that umpires cannot work with catchers is to treat them different when they are hitting. It past times — maybe 20 or 30 years ago — the catcher would get the benefit of the doubt on the marginal pitches. While you may develop a "working relationship" with the catcher on defense, you can't treat him differently than any other hitter.

Working With Hitters

While your relationship with catchers will last the whole game, and if you see a team often, you will usually get the same catcher, your relationship with hitters is much more brief.

A hitter is usually at the plate three or four times in a game for at most five or six pitches. And most of those pitches are no-brainers.

But, just as with catchers, you will find hitters that want to talk to you about a pitch. The two most common times are when they have swung at a pitch and want confirmation of where the pitch was: "If I didn't swing, was that a strike?" Or they, just like the catcher, want to discuss a called strike: "Is that as low as your zone goes?"

The first type of question is easier to deal with, because it's not argumentative. The hitter just wants to know if he made a good decision to swing. Give hitters the honest answer; more often than not, they swung at a bad pitch and just want verification.

The second question is much tougher to deal with and you can't paint yourself into a corner when they ask if that is the limit of your zone.

"I will tell them it's a good pitch," Klemm said. "If I answer that it's as far out as I go, I've put myself into a corner of where the zone is or isn't. The next pitch could be the same spot and now I've trapped myself. The hitter will always think the next one is farther out.

"It's the same way I work with catchers, but the dynamic is different because hitters are at there for three to five pitches as opposed to nine innings."

Droll completely agreed with that philosophy.

"I try to be vague," he said. "I will always answer, but it can bite you if you are too specific. I had one game where it ended with a called third strike and runners in scoring position. The kid had taken a fastball at the knees and asked where it was. I said it was right there. The next pitch: Game over. I punched him out on a pitch at the same spot."

WHAT TO WATCH
Players — either the catcher and the batter — will ask questions about pitches. Some of those conversations will be very discreet, while others will be more visible and confrontational. If a player asks a respectful question, he deserves a respectful answer in most cases. The less confrontational the umpire is, the quicker the situation will be resolved. However, if any player (including the pitcher) is making a scene, the umpire needs to take control immediately.

Working With Pitchers

Working with hitters and catchers is something that can be done very discreetly. Unless the player becomes animated or loud, usually the conversation is one that is heard by only the three people at the plate.

When a pitcher gets upset, it becomes a little more difficult. The only way you will know that a pitcher is questioning you is when he gets loud or demonstrative.

When he gets a sense of the pitcher's frustration, Uyl will rely on the catcher to shut it down.

"While I am a proponent of limited conversation with a catcher, I will use him as a conduit with the pitcher," Uyl said. "I will give the catcher the first chance to address the problem, but if he isn't working with me or can't calm the pitcher down, then I will have to address it. And when I have to address it, it could escalate quickly.

"At the high school level, I will inform the coach as well and give him a chance to address it. An umpire just can't allow the kid standing on the elevated mound in the middle of the field to be putting on a show and giving his opinion for everyone to see."

Working With Dugouts

Just as dealing with a pitcher, the conversation when it starts with a dugout will be less than discreet.

For Droll, it depends on how the conversation starts from the dugout.

"If the head coach asks a question, especially if he handles himself respectfully, I'm going to try and answer it," he said. "But we're not going to make it a common theme throughout the game. We're not back there to do play by play.

"I don't think it's good to ignore a coach unless they are going over the line. You might have to tell them that you aren't going to answer every pitch."

Klemm, especially because of the nature of the professional game, won't deal with as much.

"I'm only dealing with one person in the dugout — either the manager or pitching coach," he said. "If they are constructive, I'll respond, but I won't ever enter into an argument."

And Klemm will not leave the dirt circle to deal with a dugout. Staying in that circle is where you belong and leaves you in a non-aggressive position.

"You can do what you need to do from there," he said. "You don't need to head to the dugout in a dispute with field personnel. It's a much more neutral position to be in."

One of the most effective tools that exists in college baseball is the formal ball-strike warning. The approved rulings read:

"Balls, strikes and checked swings are not to be argued. After a warning, any player or coach who continues to argue balls, strikes or checked swings shall be ejected from the game. Umpires shall record the warning. If a coach leaves the dugout or his position to argue a ball or strike call (including a checked swing), the coach may be ejected without warning."

While it is not as codified in the NFHS or pro rulebooks, the same philosophy can apply. Try to answer a question, but if the dugout's actions turn to argument or over-the-top objection, get a warning out. Stay calm as you deliver the warning, because you want it to be clear that you are not the aggressor. If the warning doesn't stop the problem, an ejection will. But hopefully, it won't reach that level.

Chapter 6
THE
COUNT

M any different people keep track of the pitches that have been thrown, but only the plate umpire is official when it comes to how many balls and strikes have been recorded.

That doesn't mean you won't have "help" in keeping the count. There's the scoreboard, the home scorebook, the visiting scorebook, the coaches, the players and the fans. All of the people involved all think they have excellent memories and can accurately count to three on one hand and two on the other.

Keeping the Count

The plate umpire relies on others to keep the score of the game, be it the scoreboard operator or the scorebooks of the competing teams. But while those entities also keep the count, the plate umpire is solely responsible for keeping and announcing the count.

No rule set requires an indicator be used, but the minor league umpires are required to use one by their policy manual. And there's really no excuse to not have one. You are given a device to keep the count as opposed to keeping it mentally.

There are umpires who will tell you they "stay more focused" by not having an indicator, but the experts interviewed for this book were unanimous in recommending and using an indicator. "I can't imagine working the plate without one," Hiler said. "We highly recommend it at the NCAA level."

His reasoning is that there are just too many things going on.

"My point is that too many things happen in a quick moment," he said. "There's an easy opportunity for you to lose the count out there. Every plate umpire should use an indicator. Even scoreboards get mixed up. How many times do you have the scoreboard get it wrong and you end up second guessing yourself?"

Klemm said he would have never considered not using one, even though it was required.

"I would have never taken that option," he said. "I find it bogus that guys say that concentrate harder without one. What they are telling me is that they need to not use a tool in order to stay focused on the game."

Riley said that one of his partners lost his job in the minor leagues by not using one.

"Not using one got my partner in the Florida State League fired," he said. "It was in our manual that you had to use one. There's too much going on."

Uyl has seen umpires not use an indicator, but doesn't recommend it.

"I don't shudder when I see a guy without one because the guys that don't are usually more experienced than me and they've gotten used to it," he said. "But not using one requires more concentration, which means you aren't completely focused on what you should be.

"And you don't have the safety net that having an indicator provides. I can keep track when nothing is going on. But the times when we need it are when something odd happens. You have a pickoff throw that turns into a rundown with rotations or a wild pitch and a run scores. It's a valuable tool and one that should be used."

And just to be clear, the tool should only be known as an indicator. It is not a "clicker" or "counter" — both terms are sure signs of a new or amateurish sounding umpire.

Showing the Count

With scoreboards and PA announcers just about everywhere, it would be nice if umpires didn't have to show the count. But players and coaches rightfully rely on the plate umpire for that information.

So how and how often should it be done?

Mechanically, you are telling the count to the hitter and catcher, while showing it to the pitcher. Balls are always shown with the left hand, while strikes are shown with the right hand. It is important to say the count that you show, and to always show both elements. An umpire should not just put one hand up for a count that only includes one element, i.e., a three-ball, no-strike count or a no-ball, two-strike count.

It should be held up at a height the pitcher can see. For an average height umpire, doing it shoulder width and just above shoulder height is correct (PlayPic A). There is usually no reason to hold it way overhead (PlayPic B) since you are showing it mainly to the pitcher. The count should be given once the pitcher is back on the mound and looking toward the plate. If you give it before then, you are showing it to no one — people aren't paying attention. The focus returns to the plate area once the pitcher has reengaged the pitching plate and the batter is in the box.

Additionally, umpires are not players or coaches. Two is correctly demonstrated with the index and middle fingers, not the index and pinky finger. A full count is shown with fingers up (PlayPic C), not closed fists or crossed wrists (PlayPic D).

You do not need to flash the count to the dugout, coaching box, pitcher, other coaching box and other dugout. You are showing it to provide information and no pitcher wants to have to read moving hands to figure out the count.

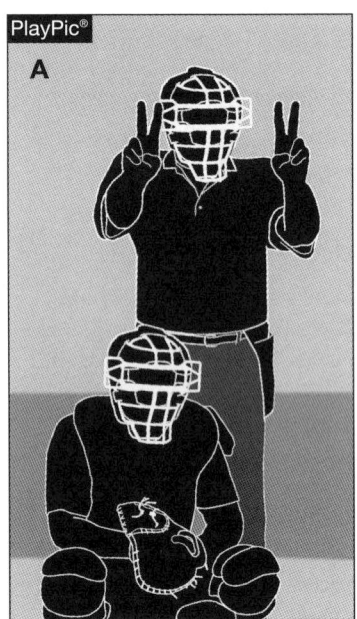

COUNT: CORRECT HEIGHT

COUNT: INCORRECT HEIGHT

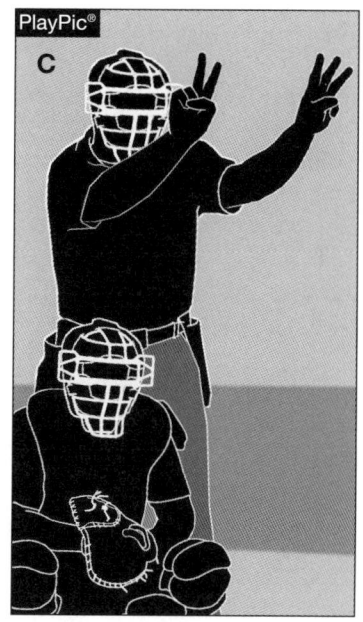

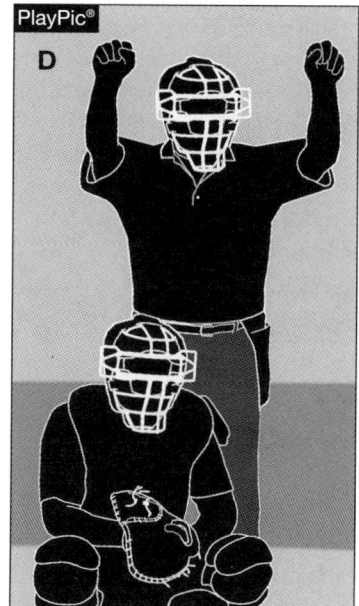

FULL COUNT: CORRECT   FULL COUNT: INCORRECT

The only time a plate umpire should vary that is when the scoreboard has it wrong. If you know where your scoreboard operator is and can get his attention verbally, but discreetly, you can say the count louder. Otherwise, hold the count up high and slightly move the hand that indicates what the scoreboard has wrong.

As for when to do it, different assigners and supervisors have different philosophies, from showing it every pitch to showing it only when it is a decision pitch — that is the at bat can end on the next pitch when the batter doesn't swing the bat (either a three-ball or two-strike count).

When Riley was actively umpiring, he would give the count after the third pitch and then after something happened.

WHAT TO WATCH
Look at the count being shown correctly and the various issues when it is shown incorrectly.

"By something happening, I mean a foul ball, a stolen base, a meeting at the mound, anything like that," he said. "That's when participants are most likely to forget it. And then I always gave it on 3-2."

Uyl and Klemm share a similar philosophy.

"I give the count the first time that we have two of anything," Uyl said. "And then again, when we get to a 3-2 count."

"I'm not opposed to doing it after each pitch," Klemm said. "But you definitely have to show it after every action."

Chapter 7
WHEN YOU ARE STRUGGLING

f you've set up in a proper stance, which includes not getting set until the catcher has made his final adjustment;

And if you've followed the ball into the mitt;

And if you've taken the time to process what you just saw before rendering your decision;

And if you've used crisp mechanics to indicate that decision …

Then you should never miss a pitch!

But every umpire who has set a goal of not missing a pitch during the course of a season has usually shattered that goal by the time the third inning of the first plate job of the season has rolled around.

Just as hitters go into long slumps or pitchers struggle to throw a strike, umpires will struggle behind the plate from time to time.

Several key things to remember when it comes to struggling: relax, figure out what you are doing wrong and correct it.
You can't go back and reverse a missed pitch, so intentionally missing another one to "even things out" is not an option.

So what can you do to right the ship?

During a Game

Unlike in some sports, such as hockey, where the action seems to never stop and you never get a chance to breathe, much less think about why you might be missing some key action, baseball is a game with plenty of natural breaks.

There is usually more than five seconds between pitches, which can be plenty of time to step back, take a deep breath and reset yourself.

According to Droll, the struggles he sees most often comes from nerves in younger umpires and bravado in veterans.

"Sometimes younger umpires get hesitant to call strikes," he said. "It's almost like they are afraid to look foolish.

"If they are working their first big series, and they haven't been around long and they want to impress, they tend to be hesitant to call a marginal strike."

When you get the sense that you are struggling, break the game down into as many little parts as possible. Forget that it's the third inning of a nine-inning game. Instead focus on just getting the next three outs. And if that doesn't do it, focus on the fact that you have to get through three outs. Finally, concentrate on just getting the next pitch correct. Nothing you do is going to change any previous calls, but focusing on one pitch, batter or inning at a time will help you turn things around.

When he gets the sense that he could be struggling, Droll said he knows what to do.

"If I feel like my timing is good, I still slow down," he said. "You can never overemphasize good timing. If I think I'm questioning myself, the first thing, I'm going to ask myself if I'm too quick. Let the pitch happen, see how the ball is presented, take your time.

"You can work yourself out of a really bad game by just making yourself slow down."

For Klemm, it's almost like returning to the first time he called pitches.

"Why is it that when I'm struggling, I don't know anybody that argues against going back to the fundamentals?" he said.

Think about the first time you were taught to call strikes. You were told to get into position when the pitcher got on the rubber, to get set as he started his delivery and then to watch the pitch all the way in and call it.

Only as you got better and more comfortable, did you ever vary from that, so keep that in mind for when you are having a rough day.

"With experience comes a freedom because you are so good at your timing that mistakes are minimized through how you stand," Klemm said.

Another way to take advantage of those natural breaks — in particular between innings, is to make eye contact with your partner. You don't have to get together for your base umpire to be able to communicate what he's seeing when he's watching you. He can tap his wrist to indicate he's talking about your timing and then either give you a thumbs up or an indication to slow down.

That can be especially helpful for a younger umpire working and wanting the support of his veteran partner. An increased level of confidence or a little suggestion can make all the difference during a game.

After the Game

Many umpires talk about the importance of the pregame conference, but when the last pitch is thrown, it's how fast can they change clothes and head to the next event in their life. That is one of the worst things you can do if you want to get better or if you want to help your partner.

A thorough postgame discussion is something that you can use to get feedback on your strike zone and mechanics related to calling balls and strikes.

Another way to get feedback after the game is to take advantage of something that wasn't very common in the past, especially at the lower levels. In all likelihood, there is going to be video of your game available somewhere.

You don't have to be working in an MLB stadium to expect a video to be available of a game. And even if there isn't a commercial broadcast of the game, there is almost always a coach or parent filming the game. Now you can't expect the camera to focus on you or to be lined up directly over the plate, but you can learn a lot by watching the video.

"I think the angles are good enough," Uyl said. "As long as the camera is in a set position, it may not give you the most accurate view of the strike zone, but it will give you a perspective that you can pick up trends and tendencies of your work and make adjustments accordingly.

"There are two extremes when we run to the video. Certainly, when you struggle, you go back and want to search for some answers. The most basic fixes often do the trick.

"But, if you have a game that you think you've been exceptional, you can enjoy watching that too, you get to feel good about yourself about the top-notch job that you did."

Appendix
HISTORY OF THE RULES

The strike zone in the *Official Baseball Rules* and all of the rules that determine strikes were different when the game began. Here's a historical look:

1876

The batter could call for a high (between the waist and shoulders), low (between the waist and one foot off the ground) or fair (either high or low) pitch. Only pitches within the requested zone counted as strikes. And if the pitcher threw nine balls – yes, nine – the batter walked. But three strikes and the batter is out was the rule of the day.

1887

Batters could no longer call their own strike zone. The strike zone was the area over the plate from the batter's knee to his shoulders. At that time, the number of balls for a walk was reduced to five, but the number of strikes for an out went up to four.

1888

The strikeout rule went back to three strikes after one season.

1889

The amount of balls for a walk is reduced to four.

1895

A foul tip became a strike.

1901

Foul balls became strikes (except when the batter had two strikes, same as today)

1950

The top of the strike zone changes to the batter's armpits and the zone is determined when the batter assumes his natural stance.

1957

A strike is defined. ""A strike is a legal pitch when so called by the umpire which (a) is struck at by the batter and is missed; (b) enters the Strike Zone in flight and is not struck at; (c) is fouled by the batter when he has less than two strikes at it; (d) is bunted foul; (e) touches the batter as he strikes at it; (f) touches the batter in flight in the Strike Zone; or (g) becomes a foul tip."

1963

The top of the strike zone returns to the batter's shoulders and the batter's zone is determined according to the batter's usual stance when he swings at a pitch.

1969

The top of the zone returns to the batter's armpits. The bottom of the zone is defined as the top of the knees, instead of just the knees. Also, the zone is determined when a batter assumes a natural stance. The umpire shall determine the strike zone according to the batter's usual stance when he swings at a pitch.

1988

The current definition for the top of the zone takes effect. "The Strike Zone is that area over home plate the upper limit of which is a horizontal line at the midpoint between the top of the shoulders and the top of the uniform pants ..."

1996

The current definition for the bottom of the zone is written, moving from the top of the knees to the bottom of the knees.

Sources: MLB.com and Baseball Almanac

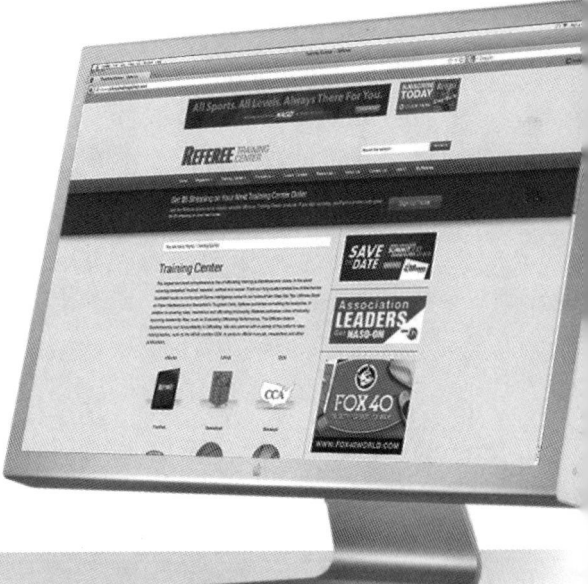